Provoking Your Faith

31 day devotional of inspired writings to encourage you

Romona K. Stromas

All rights reserved. No part of this book may be reproduced, stored, or transmitted by any means without written permission from the author/publisher, except in the case of reviews.

All scriptures taken from the Holy Bible King James Version.

Copyright © 2018 Romona K. Stromas

All rights reserved.

ISBN: 978-0-692-04290-8
ISBN-13: 978-0-692-04290-8

DEDICATION

Provoking Your Faith is dedicated to my father Mr. Willie J. Stromas and in memory of my Mother Mrs. Roberta Stromas who introduced Jesus Christ to our family. To my siblings in memory of Sheria who believed without a doubt that God has a plan for my life. My brothers Anthony and Rick, my sisters Renee, Tina, and Lisa for their prayers and support who knew by faith this day would surely come.

To my nieces, nephews, cousins, and friends thank you all for praying for me and pushing me to keep the faith when it appeared that all hope was gone. Cousin Michael Howard, you're the greatest.

To my Lord and Savior Jesus Christ thank you for blessing me and instilling within me the word of God in Philippians 1:6 Being confident of this very thing He who hath began a good work in you will perform it until the day of Jesus Christ.

Amen.

ACKNOWLEDGEMENTS

A special thank you to Elder Joyce Arnold and Min. Joyce Montgomery. Thank you both for guarding the contents of this book and for being watchmen on the wall that interceded on my behalf.

To my St. James Missionary Baptist Church Family under the leadership of Pastor Charles D. Thomas and First Lady Evangelist Lillie Thomas. I thank you all for your prayers and your love. As well as, the words of encouragement spoken over my life.

To Mrs. Deborah Gable and Ms. Chaquwonda Gable, GFab Events and Designs thank you both for supporting me and being in my corner.

To my Goddaughter Charletha Johnson and my BFF's Ra'asia Lee and Ajaia Williams thank you guys for your genuine love.

A special thank you to Ms. Gail Carter, Ms. Marolyn Evans, Mrs. Rosetta Thomas (Book Consultant and Proof Reader), and Minister Sharlene Watson for being midwives as the birth of this book came forth.

God Bless you all!

PRAYER

Heavenly Father

I come before You in the name of Jesus Christ. I thank You for the completion of this book Provoking Your Faith. It is my prayer that You will anoint every word and cause the fire of the Holy Ghost to saturate the spirit of every reader in the name of Jesus Christ. I ask that You bring forth a deeper revelation of Your word as You challenge us to rise up out of defeat as we walk in total victory that You have already given to us in the mighty name of Jesus Christ. Heavenly Father send forth insight, directions, peace, joy, strength and encouragement as only You can in the name of Jesus Christ. We thank You and we give You glory and it is done in the name of Jesus Christ.

Amen

Min. Romona K. Stromas

To contact Min. Romona Stromas

Min. Romona K. Stromas
P. O. Box 17435
Pensacola, Fl 32522

Jointheir007@yahoo.com

songwritersjoy7@gmail.com

Photographer: Mr. Ken McEady: Southfield, MI

Graphic Designer: UltraKahn22@fiverr.com

Provoking Your Faith

CONTENTS

Go Get Your Grapes   Page 11

You Can't Afford Me   Page 13

The Eulogy Of Your Pain   Page 15

Spiritual Suicide   Page 17

Stop Parking In The Graveyard   Page 19

Don't Abort Your Baby   Page 20

A Crowded Bed   Page 22

An Incarcerated Heart   Page 24

Embryo Of Time   Page 26

A Praise In Advance   Page 29

Desert Rose   Page 31

Add Extra To The Ordinary   Page 33

Step Into Your Miracle   Page 35

I Can Fly   Page 37

Remove Those Pictures From The Wall   Page 39

Transformation In The Midst Of Isolation   Page 41

Flesh Got You In And Flesh Got You Out   Page 42

The Beauty Of Midnight   Page 44

God Has Not Changed His Mind	Page 46
It's Just A Light Thang	Page 48
God's Design	Page 50
From The Pit To The Palace	Page 53
Missing The Mark	Page 55
Peace Be Still	Page 57
Sunday Experience	Page 59
Surprise	Page 61
Who Let You In?	Page 63
Your Pain Has Purpose	Page 65
Turn To The Wall	Page 67
The Wealth Of A Real Woman	Page 69
Tied of Being Comfortable	Page 71

Romona K. Stromas

GO GET YOUR GRAPES

Do you feel afraid to reach beyond the norm to get what you know God has promised you? Why is it that you allow fear to rob you of the potential of possessing your promised land? Don't be afraid of the unknown. **"Go Get Your Grapes"**.

Do you find yourself asking what if I do this or what if I do that? This is a sure sign that you are allowing fear of the unknown to dictate the path God has designed for you to take. Being fearful to take a chance in life actually minimizes the magnitude of faith that you have inside of you.

As you begin to venture into a new area of your life, walk in bold confidence knowing that you are going to accomplish exactly what you set your mind out to accomplish. Since God gave you the beginning of your vision and a glimpse of the end, then you supply the faith to believe the middle shall come to pass.

The circumstances that presently dominate the fulfillment of your promise cannot deny the power that God has already invested inside of you. You cannot succumb or submit to the spirit of fear by way of intimidation. Now is the time that you must take courage and believe in order that you may receive what God has already deemed as yours.

Keep in mind as you pursue the unknown that life is an adventure and it introduces us to something new on a daily basis. Don't you hear victory crying out in your spirit? So don't allow fear to hinder you. **"Go Get Your Grapes"**.

Deuteronomy 31:6 Be strong and of a good courage, fear not, nor be afraid of them: For the Lord thy God he it is that doth go with thee; He will not fail thee, nor forsake thee.

Isaiah 43: 1

2 Timothy 1:7

Matthew 17:20

YOU CAN'T AFFORD ME

Why do you continuously settle for relationships that are beneath your expectations? Do you find yourself attracting men you know you are unequally yoked with? Are you tired of being wined and dined as a motive to satisfy the needs of someone else as if you have a price tag upon you? It's time to take courage and you must let them know, **"You Can't Afford Me."**

We have often linked ourselves with unhealthy or unproductive relationships due to some issues from our past. We settle for relationships that we know will go no further than the nose on our faces. We have settled for fly by night love affairs and drive thru romances only to make ourselves look good to others and pacify our emotions so we won't feel alone.

Loneliness is not a curse assigned to frustrate your life. Loneliness can be viewed as an instrument designed by God to propel you to a new level of living. It is during these lonely moments we can come to realize how loving and gentle our God really is. We may not be able to realize the fullness of God's love because we are consume with searching and seeking a tangible love or a natural love.

So in the quest of seeking and searching, we get caught up in settling for whatever looks good and smell good to us. We want to impress those around us with stuff we know is worthless and that is a dangerous thing. Yes, conforming to whatever presents itself to us usually causes us to decrease the value or worth of what we expect for ourselves.

Now is the time we must realize our self-worth. Sculptured nails, pampered toes a Gucci bag and a St. John suit can be purchased. The qualities or substance that God has put on the inside of you cannot be purchased. Therefore, there is not a price tag on you and you cannot be brought. You carry the flavor and the aroma of character which is priceless.

Look up and keep stepping. Don't settle for whatever rolls your way. Know that your merchandise is good and there are some you have to let know **"You Can't Afford Me.'**

Psalms 139: 14 I will praise thee; for I am fearfully and wonderfully made.

Proverbs 31:18

1 Corinthians 7:23

THE EULOGY OF YOUR PAIN

When is enough enough? Do you wonder if God has forgotten that you are still hurting? How much pain is considered enough? Do anyone know where the scale is located to determine how much one can bear? God is the only one that knows how much you can bear. No matter what crisis you may be facing, be assured that this is **THE EULOGY OF YOUR PAIN**.

Pain is something that hurt and regardless of what type of pain you may be experiencing, too much of it can overwhelm you. Sometimes we as a people have the tendency to unconsciously undermine someone else's pain. Whether you experienced the death of a love, a divorce, child going astray or even losing your job. Pain is pain and all of it hurts.

We have to try to approach pain from a different perspective. As we go through our turmoil we can gain knowledge in many different capacities. Pain is instrumental in developing us into the soldier that God has designed for our lives. It is through our pain that we learn to stand up against the wiles of the enemy and fight back.

We can also view pain as an avenue to lead us into a boulevard of blessings. It is through this avenue that we learn to trust God in a deeper way. We began to hunger and thirst for more of Him. This dilemma will lead us into a new revelation of God. It is this pain that was divinely designed to usher you into your place of promise.

Yes, you will be just fine. God has to sometimes set us up in order to bless us. He has a plan already designed for us to fit perfectly into. Although your pain may be unbearable right now and you may have many unanswered questions concerning your situation, but pain is a temporary duty station. It is not your place of promise. You are being encouraged to change your shoes. You can kiss your woes bye-bye and put on your dancing shoes and celebrate because this is **THE EULOGY OF YOUR PAIN**.

Psalms 126:5 They that sow in tears shall reap in joy.

Psalms 119:71

Psalms 119: 67

SPIRITUAL SUICIDE

Are you sick and tired of being sick and tired? Has your present situation drained all of your joy out of you? Do you now find it comforting to do things that you know are contrary to the will of God? Although you know God is on your side, wrong doing seems quite right about now. Take a deep breath and exhale. You cannot allow temptation to destroy your destiny. You are in danger of committing **"Spiritual Suicide."**

As we listen to the news of today, suicide seems to be a very prevalent reality in our society. We even find that this horrible spirit shows no partiality to any particular race, religion, socio-economic group, sex, or age. Suicide has taken the lives of families for many centuries. Surviving family members have often been left wondering was life that hard in order for their loved ones to give up in such a manner?

As we look at this situation in the spiritual realm, can our present situation be that bad until we give up on God and the promises that He has made to us? Do you really think instant gratification will sustain the revelation of your purpose that God has unveiled to you? Don't risk it all for a moment of something that will destroy your destiny.

Yes, life is taking us down many roads that are unexplainable as well as painful. Although, God has destined us to live victoriously there is a road we cannot avoid in order to get to the boulevard of blessings. It is during this phase of our lives God can see how much trouble He can trust us with. Will we stay in the race and fight a good fight of faith, or will we abort our purpose and commit Spiritual Suicide?

It is ok to cry if you must. It is ok to kick and even scream. Don't give up on the promises that God has made nor on your dreams. Hold on to the sweet moments called possibilities knowing just as sure as God has spoken it, it shall come to pass. Do not self-inflict or kill everything that you and God has worked towards. Do not live in despair knowing you committed **"Spiritual Suicide."**

Jeremiah 29:11 For I know the thoughts that I think toward you, saith the Lord, Thoughts of peace and not of evil to give you an expected end.

1 Corinthians 10:13

Matthew 26:41

Ephesians 6:11

Galatians 5:16

STOP PARKING IN THE GRAVE YARD

Do you find it hard to let go of old issues? Are you still thinking about that old relationship you had and who your ex may be with? Are you over whelmed with grief due to the loss of a love one? Then it is time to **"Stop Parking In The Grave Yard.**

During the course of life, it is understood that there will be good times as well as bad times. We realize that pain hurts no matter what type of pain you may be dealing with. But, you must not consume yourself with old issues and allow them to frustrate the potentiality of a bright and glorious future.

The graveyard or cemetery is a permanent sleeping ground. It is not designed for you to continuously park in and remain. The struggle of a broken relationship or marriage is a pain that can ruin you, but only if you allow it to. You must learn from that situation and apply what you have learned in your next relationship and move forward.

Perhaps you yet struggle with the death of a loved one? The date of the death of your love one is not a pleasant time for you. You must learn to reflect back and be grateful for the impartation that person has made in your life. Be assured it is ok to look back, but not to remain there.

So as you continue your life from this point on, drive forward looking through your windshield and not focusing on your rearview mirror. **"Stop Parking In The Grave Yard".**

Philippians 3:13 Brethren I count not myself to have apprehended: But this one thing I do, forgetting those things which are behind, and reaching forth unto those things which are before.

Isaiah 43:18

Hebrews 12:1

DON'T ABORT YOUR BABY

Are you tied and frustrated and feel like you want to give up? Have you tried several options to conquer your frustrations only to find that there was no resolution? Well hold on a little bit longer because what you are experiencing is labor pains. God is birthing something new in your spirit. So be encouraged and **Don't Abort Your Baby.**

God has impregnated you with dreams, visions, gifts and talents that will lead you to success. The only thing about being impregnated spiritually is that impatience is a common factor that causes a premature delivery to take place.

Many are guilty of pursuing or doing things out of the season in which the Lord has designed for it to take place. Since timing is slightly off, it allows room for frustration to infiltrate the spirit and contaminate the promise.

We must allow that which is on the inside of us to grow and develop properly. Just as a fetus grow inside of its Mother's womb, we have to grow into what Jesus desires us to become. The expected time frame for a full term baby is 9 months and if something abruptly interrupts the expected due date based upon conception, the baby aborts or a miscarriage takes place.

Now that we are in a different mindset, is it possible to take God off of our time schedule and allow the beauty of time to develop or perfect us into the remarkable piece of art God created? Do not submit to frustration that's created because of impatience. Don't be anxious and **Don't Abort Your Baby.**

James 1:4 But, let patience have her perfect work, that you ye may be perfect and entire, wanting nothing.

Psalms 40:1

Romans 12:12

Romans 8:25

A CROWDED BED

When you walked away from your last relationship, did you get rid of everything they left behind? Did you change the blinds, paint the walls or purchased a brand new bed room set? Although those changes were good changes, did you release them from occupying space in your spirit or the basement of your soul? Don't rush into another relationship you are in danger of **"A Crowded Bed."**

A bed is generally known to be a resting place. If we looked at this from a natural stand point, we would immediately begin to think of a physical bed in a physical bedroom. Unfortunately, that is not the case. We must allow a deeper revelation to unveil as God begins to shampoo and filter out our spirits from things of our past.

Being married and having children has been taught to us from childhood as an ultimate goal to reach. No one plans a big wedding with the thought that one day this marriage will end in divorce. No one decide to have children from a union and suddenly you are raising the children alone. Regardless of what ended the union, hatred, resentment, and unforgiveness seems to be prime tenants that occupies ones spirit.

We then sometimes find it difficult to let go of the memory of that devastation. We paint on a big smile, we purchase expensive clothing, and we even position ourselves in the hottest spots to be chosen again. We unconsciously fail to realize our bed or our spirits are too crowded or to full with the memory and residue from our previous relationships. We must evict everything out of our spirit from our past in order to make room for the miracle God has for us.

Go ahead and serve notice to your present tenants. They will not get a 30 day notice to quit. As of right now, they must go. Our temple, our building, our soul, our bed is under new management. We will no longer submit to **"A Crowded Bed"**.

Matthew 11:28, 29 Come unto me all ye that labor and are heavy laden and I will give you rest. Take my yoke upon you and learn of me and I am meek and lowly in heart and ye shall find rest unto your souls.

2 Corinthians 5:17

Isaiah 43:18,19

Galatians 2:20

AN INCARCERATED HEART

What have you experienced so bad that has your heart incarcerated? Do you have the key to unlock your broken heart? Have you chosen to put your heart into lock down forever? God is so awesome and He has so many ways in which HE uses to restore us back to life. I know life is swell for you right now, but so much more is in store. You no longer have to live with **AN INCARCERATED HEART.**

You have been through so much pain until now you have decided to place your heart under lock and key? Are you aware of the final thing that has pushed you into confinement? You have gone through so much and now enough is just simply enough with no pain resume being needed.

Yes I too can sing in the choir stand with you. Heart ache is one of the most devastating pains you can imagine. Unlike a broken arm that is painful or a toothache that is painful, but the most tender area of our existence is injured. Sadly, but we begin to think the only way to protect it is by voluntarily placing our heart into bondage.

Your heart being placed in bondage is a trick of the enemy. The enemy will use whatever means made available to him in order to steal your joy. Somehow we have allowed life's ups and downs to super cede the liberty in which Christ gave to every believer at Calvary.

You must come to a place within yourself to defeat this spirit of deception. This false illusion of protection is robbing you of your present moment joys. If we reversed our hurt by turning it into to a learning experience, we could help others as well as ourselves.

Pain is pain and all of it hurts, but we cannot allow pain on this side of earth to still the joy Christ intends for us to experience. So let's help each other by taking authority over the spirit of deception and allow Christ to pick up the broken pieces of our heart. Today we declare freedom over **AN INCARCERATED HEART**.

John 8:36 If the son therefore shall make you free, you shall be free indeed.

Psalms 34:18

Psalms 37:4

John 14:1

THE EMBRYO OF TIME

When Lord? How much longer did you say?

As we look at the miraculous manifestation of a new born, we can conclude that God is an awesome God and only HE can bring forth creation. It is sometimes the nature of human kind to try and figure out the miraculous works of the Lord. In one's own quest or desperation to unravel the miraculous, it is very likely a new reverence and respect for the authority of God can be embrace.

Many philosophers have tried for many years to unravel or explain the phenomenon of God. Some have based their conclusions upon scriptures, but it is their own interpretation that solidifies their statements. You will also find some philosophers have no scripture basis, but their statements are merely based upon their opinions.

The era in which we live in now have tried to duplicate God's creation and call it cloning. No matter how advanced our technology becomes or how advanced we as humans acquire a certain level of education, there are many things that are too high or deep for our natural mind to perceive. God allows certain witty inventions to take place or come forth into existence as the time changes. However, HIS miraculous powers cannot be unraveled or explained. Therefore, miracles or wonders is the appropriate term that signifies the experience many have witnessed. There is no humanistic explanation or philosophical interpretation that can explain such a divine revelation of God's power and authority.

As we look at conception. We find that in order for a woman to become impregnated, she must be able to conceive or receive the seed from the male that is being placed into her body. Once conception has taken place, the seed is now inside of the womb or uterus developing or growing **as time takes its natural course.** Time is that area in our lives that many of us seem to have very little of. We must be able to look at time in a double meaning. Time can be looked at from a kronos perspective. Kronos denotes a space in time such as long or short. But kairos has a fixed or definite period a set time or appointed time. It is during pregnancy that time appears to be your worst enemy. All because your physician has given to you a due date for your delivery and it is taking time to long for your turn to arrive.

As we look at Kairos, we can see that God has a set time or an appointed time for this delivery to come forth. He is the only one that knows the totality of the embryo that lies within one's womb. Our blessings, our miracles, our personal requests that we have made known to the Lord has not been over looked neither are they forgotten. Those requests are yet being developed, nurtured, cultivated and prepared in the embryo of time. As time takes it natural course, allow God to complete the things that only He know needs to be completed on both ends of the requests. He can then allow a kairos moment to take place in your life. Yes because HE is God. He controls time.

So rest in the assurance of knowing when God has spoken something over your life, take Him off of your time schedule. Allow Him to work by His timing. We can give God praise over the revelation way before the manifestation or the delivery of our request. Just knowing HE has spoken it and it will come to pass.

Regardless of what your vision or your dream is, guard the womb of your spirit so that you will not allow contamination to cause you to miscarry or abort what is in side of you.

Your baby, your desires, your vision, your new business is what God is entrusting you with as you share with others to encourage them to push towards there delivery date. God is yet on your side. Your request is in **THE EMBRYO OF TIME.**

Job 14:14   All the days of my appointed time will I wait until my change come.

Psalms 27:13, 14

Isaiah 40:31

A PRAISE IN ADVANCE

How long have you waited for something great to happen in your life? Do you find no matter how long it takes, you still cannot give up? Did you dream of having your own business or becoming a housewife, a Mother or Father one day? Have you lost your expectations? I know all of those things seemed impossible. They appeared to far fetch for you to accomplish. Well perhaps, your timing was not God's timing. Don't give up on your expectations. Stir up your anticipation and give God **A PRAISE IN ADVANCE.**

I remember growing up as a child, how my parents loved the convenience of owning their own garden. Mom and Dad took great pleasure in tilling the ground. They prepped and prepared the soil as they planted different types of seeds into the ground. I would watch as they took turns going to check and see if what they had planted had come forth.

Although, the grounds had been properly prepped, weeds would somehow outgrow the seeds that had been planted. Now it was time to filter out or cut away those things that did not belong in the garden. Sometimes it would take months before anything would sprout up, but my parents did not give up. They placed a stick in the garden and placed the package that the seeds came in on top of the stick. This picture was a snap shot of what was to come forth as proper planting and watering instructions had taken place.

Our lives can be compared to that of a garden. We have to allow the Lord to prep and prepare us for what it is that we are asking. Sometimes we pray for things not realizing that others are also involved. The blessing will come and with that blessing responsibility and accountability will be attached. As the Lord the Keeper of the garden or our soul, monitors, feeds, water, and increases our lives as HE sees we are ready to handle what we are asking for.

It is not HIS desire for us to give up or lose expectations for what we are seeking. We have to pray or make our petition known to HIM and rest in it. It is HE that placed the desire inside of us because HE wants us to be all that HE has destined us to be. Yes life gets difficult at times and yes you lose faith, but it is ok. You lost faith only to gain a new level of faith. The faith you had was good for that level that you were once at. Now it takes a new level of faith to push you to expect even when you don't have the anticipation to do.

Now after time as taken its course, the seeds planted begins to bud. Yes that desire inside of you is seed. The seed required instructions, watering, nurturing, struggles, pains, tender loving care and THE SON'S LIGHT to yield it's desired produce. Regardless if you do not see any natural indication that God has your request or the seed inside of you on HIS mind, hold on to your snap shot. Hold on to your faith. Hold on to your expectations and your anticipation because the bud is an indication that your blessing is on the way. Give God **A Praise In Advance.**

Job 14: 8, 9 It's roots may grow old in the ground and its stump die in the soil, v9 yet at the scent of water it will bud and put forth shoots like a plant.

Psalms 9:1

Psalms 34:1

Habakkuk 2:3

DESERT ROSE

Have you ever been faced with a situation and felt you were in it all alone? You sit back and wonder how did you end up in this place that you are now in? Although you know God is with you as you face this battle, for some reason you cannot sense His presence. Please don't let go of your faith now. You have been summoned to this place of solitude and you will be just fine. You will graduate with honors as a **DESERT ROSE.**

Here you are in this isolated, empty, and seemingly dry place in your life. I know you are not sure what happened or how you even landed in such a dismal area of your spiritual walk. Discouragement has shattered the burning desires within you to reach for deeper depths and higher heights.

Discouragement has a way of affecting the most powerful and faithful individuals in life. It is during these times, God seizes the opportunity with in all of us to show Himself bigger than what we imagine or thought Him to be. This time of barrenness or abandonment is really preparation for a promotion.

In the book of Exodus, God called Moses to come to the back of the mountain and go through an intense preparation for what was before him. God is sovereign and almighty, therefore He knows what is ahead of us way before He send or place us in a specific position. God realized that Moses had insecurities and he was very compassionate towards people. Those qualities are not necessarily bad qualities. Those qualities could have hindered the call later that God had upon Moses life.

Moses received education while in Pharaoh's court, but that was not sufficient enough for the call God placed upon his life. Therefore, solitude, hardship, gloom, and being brokenhearted was actually training and preparation for the promotion that God desired to grant unto to Moses. There was something far greater ahead than the present locality of Moses mentality.

Your Sahara desert is not your permanent residency. As you temporarily pass through this phase of your life, you will learn and experience God in a depth that you did not know of beforehand. Many things can be taught, but only experience can bring forth a revelation of God in a deeper way.

You are under the providential or continual care of the Father. He hears your cries, feels your pain, and He understands your dilemmas. Rest my love and close your eyes. Look suddenly, a full bloomed rose arrived. Silence is not abandonment. Stillness does not mean God is not working in your favor. You were being prepared for a promotion that required wilderness training. You have graduated with honors as a **Desert Rose.**

ROMANS 8:32 He that spared not his own son, but delivered him up for us all, how shall He not with Him also freely give us all things.

Hosea 13:5

Psalms 147:3

Isaiah 35:1

ADD EXTRA TO THE ORDINARY

Are you tired of doing things the same old way? Do you find that your surroundings have become too close for comfort? Although, you are grateful for the things you do have, do you find that something about ordinary has you sick to the stomach? Even the job you once loved so much now seems to be like old soup to you. The same thing all over and the rich flavor it once had is no longer there. You are bored. It is time to **ADD EXTRA TO THE ORDINARY.**

There are times when we are excited about a move, a job, a new marriage or even a new church. We have the opportunity to meet and greet. We now have new people and new ideas to share with each other. We can even open up our hearts and minds to learn from other people experiences as we continue this new adventure.

After we have invested valuable time in many areas of our lives, we can sometimes become frustrated. Often in a marriage when this happens, other unacceptable avenues are taken to satisfy spontaneous adventure. In one's effort to satisfy this crave, families are torn apart, shame creeps into the picture and many hearts are left broken for no legitimate reason.

Now you are in this place called ordinary, a common place, a place of habit and not productivity. You are inviting trouble to cruse into your territory for foul play. Your mind is your territory and you have to protect that at all cost. Many do not like to admit it, but the devil's workshop is an idle mind. If you allow your mind to become inactive or lazy your life will be just a matter of course and not an exciting adventure.

Doing things in an ordinary way or customary way is not a bad thing. If we looked at a church's order of service, it is a beautiful thing to have structure. We can anticipate the next move of the suggested flow of service. The choir knows when to sing, the deacons know their time to pray, the hymn of the morning is neatly placed and the preacher know when it is time for the message to be proclaimed. What happens if the Holy Spirit shows up unannounced, not typed in on the order of service, and demands just worship? Do you think HE just wants to disrupt the order of service or add another facet to the ordinary order of service?

Our lives can be viewed the same way. We have established a set order of the day. We have established what time to get up, what time to prepare breakfast, and what route to take to get to work. Now we are just simply bored and God is prepping us for a major move in our lives. Commonalty or sameness has to become prevalent before we realize we need to push for bigger and better things. We can come up with one hundred and ten reasons to remain comfortable and not step out and pursue the greater things that's hidden inside of us. Out of the one hundred and ten reasons, the biggest question is what if?

We cannot continuously sit on a job for ten to fifteen years knowing it is a dead end and remain complacent. Even in the church setting, some churches are fueling stations. They are designed to meet the need in your spiritual walk for that period of time. After your spirit has been serviced from that station, move forward into the things that God has spoken over your life. Do not feel bad because your spiritual hospitalization for that hospital has ended? Greatness is sneaking out of you and others around you can see it. You are not aware of it because you have gotten a little comfortable with the ordinary way of doing things.

Ordinary is not a negative term. Ordinary is what God implemented in order for something greater to emerge in your life. Structure, discipline, what to do, and what not to do was all a part of the plan to produce the super that is now being added to the natural inside of you. So rejoice. You have graduated to a new level of living a new level in your spirituality. Don't curse ordinary **ADD EXTRA TO THE ORDINARY.**

Matthew 25:23 His Lord said unto Him well done good and faithful servant; thou hast been faithful over a few things, I will make thee ruler over many things enter into the joy of the Lord.

Psalms 75: 6, 7

STEP INTO YOUR MIRACLE

Did you have your plans all in order and suddenly it fell apart? How did something so very simple turn into total chaos in your life? Do you feel as though your entire world has tumbled down? Are you looking at all the broken pieces of your life and yet trying to figure out where to start to put them back together? Perhaps God does not want you to put them back together. He wants you to **STEP INTO YOUR MIRACLE.**

So you got up this morning expecting a normal day and suddenly your entire world was shaken. It is so very difficult to comprehend or try to understand why the rug was snatched from under you. It would be easier to accept turmoil had your life displayed total displeasure from the Lord. You have been a good friend to those on your job as well as in your church. You have taken care of your family to the best of your abilities and whenever anyone asked you to do anything you were there.

It is so easy for us to accept trouble or turmoil when we think we have done something wrong. We are sometimes taught bad experiences are the result of God punishing us for doing something wrong. Yes, the bible does teach us that God does punishes sin. Did you ever think God maybe up to something else and He has not revealed that to you at this point what that is?

The Lord has to take us through certain experiences in life in order that we open up our minds and allow a new revelation of Him to be revealed. We cannot go through life believing God for only one area or aspect in our walk. Therefore, HE has to reveal Himself to us through revelations. As you experience different things in your life, you now need the Lord in a different capacity. By needing Him in a different capacity, your mind can hold or grasp that area HE has evolved in as you make room for Him to do that.

So the broken pieces of your life that's crumbling around you is the Lord's doing. He's shaking up the fallow ground of your spirit and prepping it for a supernatural move that only HE can do. Your walk before the Lord is pleasing and now is the perfect time for HIM to disrupt your plans and bless you. Your blessing is wrapped in disguise as chaos and turmoil. Chaos and turmoil slowed you down, snatched your attention into a total different place, and now you're spirit has the capacity to house a supernatural revelation of the Lord. You are now on miracle territory. Your spirit is in the company of the miraculous. **STEP INTO YOUR MIRACLE.**

ACTS 3:7 And he took him by the right hand, and lifted him up: and immediately his feet and ankle bones received strength. V8 And he leaping up stood and walked, and entered with them into the temple, walking, and leaping and praising God.

Mark 8:23

Matthew 19: 26

I CAN FLY

Have you tried to accomplish some things in your life and everyone around you has tried to discourage you? Do you know if you can accomplish that deep desire within your heart based upon your own speculations or is it fear? Do you know why you have allowed your surroundings to dictate your future? Throw yourself out of the nest and yell out **"I CAN FLY"**.

Have you allowed yourself to remain in the comfort zone of your surroundings to long? I know how you feel. Now you want to move forward, but everyone around you is trying to pull you backwards instead of encouraging you to press forward and pursue your goals. Don't allow yourself to remain in the crab basket no more. It is time to press, push, and pull within your own self until you have propelled yourself to the place of promise.

The nest often referred to as a home, a safety place, or a place of rest for certain types of birds. This home or nest is not a place where the birds are expected to live or dwell until death due them part. Even in our lives from a natural perspective, we are not to live or dwell in a nest of comfort based upon others nor our surroundings. The nest, although it's a place of safety, can also be a hindrance to one fulfilling its deepest desires.

Once your mind and your spirit have conceived the fact to go beyond the norm, trouble will surely knock at your door. Trouble is often disguised as advice or wise counsel. Please be careful of this type of counsel "are you sure about that", if it was me", or "why do you want to do that". Those are warning signs of a negative seed to be imparted in your spirit and hold you back in the nest of comfort with everyone else. You must guard your ear gates and your eye gates. Do not become consumed with the neighborhood of do nothings and launch out of the nest, go beyond, and do something.

I am sure you are aware of the crab mentality. You do not have to become a fatality of that mentality. Many times we are excited about goals and desires we would like to achieve and we share this with others. You cannot share your aspirations with people that have retired in the nest of comfort and love it there. They will not understand nor encourage you to soar. You can yet love them, but from a distance to prevent a crab mentality fatality.

Don't worry about the opinions from no one because God has destined you for greatness. He will hide you from the opinions of others until you realize you can move forward without being afraid. Trust me, the old neighborhood and the nest of comfort knew it all along. Go ahead and stretch forward. Kick yourself out of the nest of comfort and yell out **"I CAN FLY"**.

Psalms 18:36 Thou has enlarged my steps under me, that my feet did not slip.

Romans 8:37

2 Corinthians 2:14

"REMOVE THOSE PICTURES FROM THE WALL"

Do you find yourself walking in the mall and suddenly something or someone reminds you of a bad experience from your past? No matter how many times you have chosen to start over, you still feel a tugging inside that pulls you backwards and not forward? How long are you going to continue to dwell on the" has been" and reach for what "can be"? It's time to **"REMOVE THOSE PICTURES FROM THE WALL."**

No matter how we try to deny the hurt from our past, somehow it has a way of creeping out of the cracks of our inner most being. Our past is an area that we will never be able to change. It is up to us to learn from our past and pursue our future with a spirit of expectation.

If we focused on a home being built in the natural, the furnishings of the new home and the pictures that will go on the wall are the final touches before the big house warming celebration. If we tried to place new pictures on top of old pictures, we will destroy the new molding. The beauty of the new pictures will not be appreciated because the old ones have obscured or hidden the potential the new pictures possess.

The painful memories of your past are like old pictures hanging on the wall of a new home. You have changed everything on the outside, but the wall of your spirit still has old pictures of inner or hidden pain. Do not continue to live in your pain for pain was never designed by God for you to dwell or live there.

Be assured that sometimes the pain we experience in life is necessary or instrumental as God develop us to be all that He has destined us to be. You have thrown the person, the place, and the thing out, so why not throw out the memory as well? **"REMOVE THOSE PICTURES FROM THE WALL."**

Romans 8:28 And we know that all things work together for good to them that love God, to them who are the called according to his purpose.

2 Corinthians 5:17

Luke 9:62

TRANSFORMATION IN THE MIDST OF ISOLATION

Why does God continuously call you to a place of isolation? You have such a drive to win souls and to help others, but yet you hear solitude is best for you. Don't give up and don't lose hope. God is preparing you so he can present you to the nations. Enjoy this time alone with Him as you receive a **"Transformation In The Midst Of Isolation."**

Loneliness has often been associated with a negative connotation. When we refer to loneliness, we are often made to feel left out or not accepted by others. However, being in a place of loneliness allows God room to speak to our hearts and mind without interruptions.

You must keep in mind it is ok to enjoy life surrounded by others, but there are times God will summon or call you to a place of stillness or loneliness in order to impregnate your spirit with his word, will, and desires for your life. We all are guilty of clinging onto ideas and words spoken to us by others. Please remember there are some words that God Himself desires to speak directly into you.

As you continue to grow and mature spiritually, don't view loneliness as a curse. Embrace it and appreciate it. God needs this time alone with you and Him as He transforms you into what he desires you to be. This moment you have alone with God will soon pass away. Your life is soon to be filled with a greater responsibility. So allow this revelation of loneliness to prepare you for your **"Transformation In The Midst Of Isolation."**

ISAIAH 51:2 Look unto Abraham your Father and Sarah that bare you: For I called them alone and blessed him and increased him. Genesis 12:1,2

Hebrews 11:1

Galatians 6:9

FLESH GOT YOU IN AND FLESH GOT YOU PUT OUT

During those moments when we are vulnerable, why does the enemy attack us the hardest? Even after we know it is the enemy, why do we still allow him room to set up camp in our hearts? No matter how saved we are, we are still human. We have feelings and emotions. However, we do not have to give place to our flesh. Hear ye hear ye I have an announcement to make **"Flesh Got You In And Flesh Got You Put Out"**.

As we deal with the ups and downs of life, we often find ourselves thinking and doing things way out of our character. Dealing with the stresses of life can sometimes make us feel as though God has left us sailing on a lonely sea all by ourselves.

The enemy then begins setting up doubt in our mind. We even question ourselves "has God forgot about us", or "why am I fighting here all alone"? Now in your quest for answers to your questions or someone to reassure you that God is there, the enemy sneaks in through an area of your life that has not received closure and preys on your vulnerability.

We must realize that we are human and humans react to situations in a fleshly manner. Therefore our feelings and emotions begin to rule our minds and where our mind goes, so does our behavior. We must be careful to embrace God's Word and not the person that is speaking the Word because a spirit of deception is always waiting to prey on a vulnerable individual.

From this point on, please remember that flesh is a battle that we will fight until Christ returns. Therefore, feed your spirit, your mind, and your heart God's Word and the Word will fight for you even when you don't have the strength to fight for yourself. So pick yourself up from the pit you are in and work the Word that is buried inside of you. Crucify your flesh daily and speak boldly to the enemy **"Flesh Got You In And Flesh Got You Put Out."**

Romans 8:13 For if you live after the flesh you will die: but if ye through the spirit do mortify the deeds of the body, ye shall live.

Galatians 6:8

Romans 8:8

THE BEAUTY OF MIDNIGHT

How long does midnight last? Does your life feel like a midnight rendezvous or midnight madness? Does your life feel like a dark tunnel with no ending? When does the midnight moment in a person's life find a conclusion? Perhaps you are facing something traumatic in your life, but did you know midnight last only a minute. Stay tune because you are about to behold **THE BEAUTY OF MIDNIGHT.**

Everyone in life experience's trying times. There is something about struggles and pain that links all races, religions, and the opposite sex into one category. We all experience hard times and find different avenues to conclude why such struggle may be present in our lives.

These difficult moments or trying moments can be identified or compared to what some call midnight madness. Midnight was never designed to be a time considered as a tragic. Although it is identified as being situated between extremes, we can decide how or what midnight will be in our lives on an individual basis. By being situated between extremes, we can trust our faith to propel us to the precious place we desire. We must be able to hold on because midnight is a momentary experience.

So your situation, your turmoil, your loss is not an everlasting moment forever and ever amen. It is a moment in time designed, designated and orchestrated by the Lord. Our midnight experiences are times that God is allowed to step into an opportunity and magnify His sovereignty into our lives. We must be willing to trust

Him even when there is no physical evidence that He is working or moving on our behalf.

Our faith in God has to assure us that He is in total control and this midnight moment will not cause us to drift back into the bad taste of defeatism. We must know and stand on the authority of God's word in spite of what our natural eye reveals. Our faith that is spirituality when connected with the womb of our spirit brings forth actuality. We cannot focus on the situation, but we have to see or view ourselves as the victors that Christ has deemed us to be.

So don't fret your midnight moment. It is the time for something new to emerge. Speak seeds of faith while you are between extremes. Midnight last ONLY but one minute and then it is time for something new to emerge. Inhale and exhale you are about to behold **THE BEAUTY OF MIDNIGHT**.

Psalms 30:5 Weeping may endure for a night, but joy cometh in the morning.

1Peter 4: 12

Proverbs 18:10

2 Corinthians 4:17

GOD HAS NOT CHANGED HIS MIND

How long have you been waiting for the manifestation of some promises you know God has spoken to you? Do you find it easier to walk away than to press and preserve until the end? Why does it seem that those around you are receiving their promises, but you have not? Don't give up just yet. **God Has Not Changed His Mind.**

Holding on to the promises of God can sometimes be a very lonely walk. Sometimes were more discouraged than encouraged. But we must realize that a season of waiting is not to punish us, but to perfect us as God prepare us for the promises that He has spoken.

Our waiting season does not mean God has closed the doors on that in which He has spoken. We must allow Him to work in us as He deposits into us the things in which He desires to come out of us. Although this is a process, it is perfected through time.

Time is not our worst enemy. It is through time that God manifests His promises. He can manifest them instantly or He can manifest them over a period of time. But we have to supply the faith in the midst of the process.

In the book of Genesis Chapter 18, God promised Abraham and Sarah a child. Sarah was in disbelief because she looked at this miracle from God in the natural. Her medical record did not line up with the promise that God had spoken. She was well stricken in age. But regardless of her self-evaluation, God's word prevailed.

So regardless of life's obstacles and your self-evaluation, your promises shall still emerge. Be careful not to doubt in the midst of the making of your miracle, but grab a hold of your faith. Trust the very thing God has spoken over your life because "**God Has Not Changed His Mind**".

2 Corinthians 1:20 For all the promises in Him are yea, and in Him Amen unto the glory of God by us.

2 Peter 3:9

Habakkuk 2:3

IT'S JUST A LIGHT THANG

How long are you going to walk around wearied and depressed over matters that you cannot solve on your own? Will you continue to call your family and friends seeking an answer, knowing in reality you are even more confused than before? Stop spinning your wheels. Give those concerns over to Jesus because to Him**, IT'S JUST A LIGHT THANG!!!**

Life often brings situations that are trying to our faith. Unfortunately our faith is made stronger through our troubled times. It is doing these trying times that we can exercise our trust system and relax in the assurance that God is working on our behalf.

Trouble has a way of dimming the possibility of the potential that lies dormant inside of us. Therefore no matter what comes our way, we must continue to seek God to lead us and guide us through this wilderness period. Tough times were never meant to destroy us, but to strengthen us, cultivate us and develop us spiritually.

Although it is God's desire for us to be strong, we must not become self-reliant and deny Him the seat of authority to operate in our lives. Being strong willed hinders God from fixing our problems. We are actually telling God to step back because we can fix it. In our quest to fix it, we become over whelmed because we do not want to admit that the problem is too much for us to handle.

Did you know this is exactly where God desires us to be? In this place of brokenness, God can speak to us clearly and filter out the many voices we have allowed to crowd our minds. It is ok to relax in the arms of Jesus. It is ok to rest in the full assurance that when we are weak, God is yet strong. Be assured our troubled times are not too much for God to handle. Give it over to Him.
"IT'S JUST A LIGHT THANG"!

2 Corinthians 12: 9 And He said unto me, My grace is sufficient for thee: for my strength is made perfect in weakness.

1 Peter 5:7

Matthew 11:28

GOD'S DESIGN

Have you ever tried to make something without following a pattern? Is it ok to skip instructions before you bake something you have never baked before? Do you think that you can look at the outside of something and conclude what it contains within? No may be appropriate for all of the above questions. Therefore, we must be careful that we are not superficially charmed on the outer and lack God's instructions within. Seek to be **God's Design**.

Have you ever found yourself looking at something and then say I can make that? Many times we all are guilty of trying to duplicate something we like. I can remember watching my Mother bake sweet potato pies and add all of the ingredients by memory. I am yet trying to conquer that great taste in that pie that she was able to master so very well. I have checked and rechecked to see if I left out some of the ingredients, but to my surprise I had not.

I finally came to the conclusion that Mom gave me a pattern to follow. She gave to me a recipe that contained ingredients and instructions. It was up to me to listen to those instructions and abide by the order in which she gave to me. Perhaps if I had practiced more in the order in which the foundation for the pie was laid, I could then venture into my own avenue and explore different flavors to add to the foundation that was established.

As we look at our spiritual life, it can be view from the same perspective. We sometimes look at a person of faith and decide we want to be like that person. Many have said I want to pray like so and so. We have to realize that a person of faith exemplifies a life of pain, sacrifice, and many tears. We are not so privileged to know the ends and outs of the midnight hour. It is because many only see the morning glory and they are not enlightened by the entire story.

It is a beautiful thing to view others in the faith whether naturally or biblically, but always remember it took divine instructions to propel those into that promised place. God has spoken too many through divine inspirations to lead and guide all of us. The Word of God is our foundation and it contains all the necessary ingredients needed to live a victorious life. We must have an ear to listen and not just hear instruction.

As we listen to divine instructions, we yield to what is being said to us. We have to be careful not to allow good sound advice or instructions to fall upon deaf ears because we already heard that before. We already did that before. Keeping in mind that there is nothing new falling from the sky. The same Word of God still remains the same, but has different views based upon the instructions the writer received. Do we open our minds and hearts to any and everything? Of course not, but the bible says to try the spirit by the spirit and see if it be of God.

We must remain open and receptive to instructions by using wisdom. Wisdom is the principal, the essential or important thing. Wisdom is that area that opens our mind and our heart up to receive instructions. Many try to give instructions, but those without wisdom have chosen not to adhere to it.

As I mentioned the sweet potato pie, I had instructions but not wisdom. Mom knew how much each ingredient meant to the success of the pie. She did not have to follow line by line in order for the success of this pie to unfold. The wisdom she possessed and the experience in preparing the pie qualified her to flow by memory and not a written recipe. The fact that she obtained instructions early on from her Mother and followed the pattern she gave to her equipped her to venture out and add her own ingredients to the same recipe.

God has given to us a pattern to follow. It is up to us to study His word and to allow His ingredients to develop us into what HE desires for our life. Many of us desire to be examples of men and women of faith, worship leaders, preachers or teachers, but we must allow God to design us with proper instructions before being on full display. We cannot risk our reputation or character being displayed without God's instructions. Allow God to instruct because HIS instructions will sustain the foundation of your soul regardless of what you may encounter. Receive instructions and become **God's Design.**

Proverbs 2:6 For the Lord giveth wisdom and from His mouth came knowledge and understanding.

Proverbs 7:4

FROM THE PIT TO THE PALACE

Have you ever wondered why it seems as though you can never get out of the rut you're in? Have you ever wondered, if this place was designed by God? I know the pit is not a place in which one would consider a mountain top experience. However, in order for one to appreciate the mountain top, one must experience the valley lows. Hold on and remain steadfast. You are in transition **"From The Pit To The Palace"**.

Wouldn't it be so nice if we had specific answers for all the questions that pondered our minds? We all know one of the main questions we ask God is why? We have a tendency to make ourselves believe if we knew "why" this or that it would somehow make the process or the pit experience a little easier to endure.

Well unfortunately life does not give to us answers to our situations instantaneously. There are things that will be revealed a little here and a little there. We must take courage and believe Jesus has already worked the situation out for our good. We must not consume our thoughts with seeds of defeat, but we must feed our thoughts with seeds of faith.

As we view the story of Joseph, we find his pit experience ultimately led him to the palace. Now as we focus on the pit or valley low that we are presently enduring, we must believe that God has designed a greater purpose for our lives and the pit is a part of the process in order for the promise to be revealed.

Don't curse your pit. It is only a temporary duty station. The training, the pruning, the cultivating, the development, character building or fanning the inner flame within you is necessary for your arrival at the palace. Yes, God has you exactly where he wants you for this appointed time. He is preparing you to meet him. The greatest reward of any pit or situations you face is, knowing you are being prepped to meet the King. Stay in and fight you are in transition **"From The Pit To The Palace"**.

Psalm 105:19 Until the time that his word came: the word of the Lord tried him.

Exodus 2:24

Psalms 23:4

MISSING THE MARK

Have you made some mistakes in life that seems hard to shake? Do you feel like God cannot use you because you keep making the same mistakes over and over again? Stop condemning yourself. God is a loving and patient God. He does not see you for where you are, but for what you shall become. The truth of the matter is, we all are guilty of **Missing the Mark.**

Missing the mark or making mistakes in life is an area we all have experienced. The sad thing is we allow it to throw us into a state of isolation. Yes, many hide themselves in this place because of the guilt and shame that's associated with the mistakes that have been made and will not trust God for their total deliverance.

But, you have to be careful because the enemy will then began to have a field day with your mind. He will try and make you think God is not with you and He cannot use you because of your flaws. It's important to realize, your flaws are not who you are. It's just a weakness that the grace of God can heal as you trust Him.

Someone may be wondering, why do I continuously make the same mistakes? This may be happening because the enemy has a stronghold on that particular area of your life. Therefore, you have to attack it in the spirit by using the word of God. 2 Cor. 10:4 says for the weapons of our warfare are not carnal. They are not of this world. But, mighty through God to the pulling down of strongholds.

Utilize the power of God that is on the inside and you. You are more than a conqueror. Do not sit back passively and allow the enemy to torment you. Fight back and trust God to perfect those things that are on the inside of you. You do not have to keep **Missing The Mark.**

1 John 1:9 If we confess our sins, God is faithful and just to forgive us of our sins and cleanse us of all unrighteousness.

Colossians 1:14

Romans 3:24

Romans 8:1

PEACE BE STILL

Have you ever encountered so many storms in life until you didn't know what to do? Did it seem as though the turmoil would never come to an end? Many times we are faced with challenging times and it can appear as though God is not there with us. But just when we want to throw in the towel, suddenly we hear a stilled small voice speak **Peace Be Still**.

Life can often take us thru many challenges that appear to be impossible to solve. These challenges seem to appear at the most inappropriate time. If we knew our marriage would fall to pieces as a detrimental sickness hit our body, we might be more prepared to deal with the consequences of the storm.

But since it showed up like scatter showers that progressed into a category 5 hurricane, we are now more vulnerable to the winds and the rains that come with the storm. Yes, it's during these times that we must trust God when we don't see what He's doing in our lives. We have to trust God when we don't understand the plan He has for our lives.

The storms that we face are designed by God to develop us into the vessel He desires us to become. Becoming often involves challenges and challenges tests our faith. But it is imperative that we understand these storms that we face can frustrate our progress, but they cannot stop our purpose.

So I encourage you as I encourage myself to weather thru the storms of life. For they have come to make us not to destroy us. With stand your trials and test. Speak over your lives and declare **Peace Be Still.**

Mark 4:39 And he arose and rebuked the wind and said unto the sea, peace be still. And the wind ceased, and there was a great calm.

Colossians 3:15

Psalms 29:11

Proverbs 3: 5, 6

SUNDAY EXPERIENCE

Have you experienced so much on this week and now you can't wait until Sunday morning service comes? You know if you make it to Sunday morning, everything will be all right. Has the devil taken his best shot at you and now you need the encouragement from the Sunday worship experience to carry you through? When life has beaten you down and no friend you can find, we have been taught to rise up and run to the well to enjoy a **"Sunday Experience"**.

Sunday morning worship service is a part of our culture that we have known to embrace very strongly. Our traditional religious beliefs handed down from our ancestors have taught us to run to the church and tell God all about our troubles.
The praises given to God was encouraged regardless if money was in the bank or food was on the table.

As we entered into the church doors, a feeling of relief over whelmed us. Our hearts raced as we anticipated God to speak a word to our situation. This word we so eagerly waited for would soon come, but who would deliver it? Would it be the Sunday school teacher, the choir, or the Preacher? All I know is that making it to the Sunday morning experience would give us what we needed.

It is now Thursday and you are facing turmoil. You don't know if you can make it to Sunday morning to experience a move of God with the assistance of a worship service. God is coming down your street on today with a new revelation. It is time to change your Sunday experience into a SON DAY EXPERIENCE. Jesus can step into whatever is troubling you whenever you allow HIM to. He is not limited to any particular time, month of the year, nor day of the week. He is waiting for you.

As you go forward from this day continue to fellowship on Sunday morning. However, when your soul is thirsty and needs a fresh glass of water, I recommend you to the fountain of life Jesus Christ. He is the SON DAY experience. Don't limit HIM to a **"Sunday Experience"**.

I Corinthians 2:9 Eye that not seen nor ear heard, neither have entered into the heart of man, the things which God hath prepared for them that love Him.

Isaiah 64:4

SURPRISE

Are you expecting a big present for your birthday or is it a special holiday? Why have you allowed yourself to think gifts only come to you when you expect them too. Have you sat back and realize that God is up to something and He is the only one that will be able to say **"SURPRISE"**.

There are times when we feel we deserve special treats. Birthdays and holidays are prime times to show your love towards your love ones. We must come to realize that every day is a great opportunity to show our love for others. We must take advantage of the time that we have now and maximize it.

Even in our spiritual walk, we are taught to sow seeds into the kingdom. Sowing seed is not a plan designed by leaders to manipulate it's congregation to satisfy their greed. Sowing is a biblical truth. If we viewed the life of a farmer, we would see the farmer plants seeds into the ground, waters the planted seed, cultivate the seed, and move on. The farmer does not sit in the garden and wait for a bud to spring forth before he believes that seed will bring forth fruit. He plants in faith and trust God for the fruit to come forth.

As we sow into God's kingdom, only HE knows when our fruit or harvest shall spring forth. Many believers have chosen to accept certain portions of the Word of God. Sowing is an area that many debates due to the mishandling and mismanagement of money in the church setting. It is extremely important that we realize our seed is not being given to the Pastor, the Evangelist, the Prophet and no one else. Our seed is being given to that ministry of the Gospel in the name of Jesus Christ.

We cannot buy a blessing from the Lord, but we can contribute to spreading the good news as we exercise biblical principles of sowing and reaping. Just as the farmer, he knows not when the seed that has been planted is going to bud. As we obey God's laws and statures, He has the option to cause the seed or crop we have planted to yield.

Yes things have been a bit hard and you have not had as much to contribute to the ministry as you would like. Don't sweat it. Your labor has not been in vain and neither is it in vain now. You cannot keep your own score based upon what you think you did or did not do and reward yourself. The eyes of the Lord is upon you and HE is stopping by to let you know it is harvest time. Yield vessel eat the fruit of your labor. Receive your **'SURPRISE !!!**

I Corinthians 15:58 Therefore my beloved brethren be ye steadfast and unmovable always abounding in the work of the Lord fore as much as ye know that your labor is not in vain in the Lord.

I Corinthians 3:6

Galatians 6, 7

1 Corinthians 2:9

WHO LET YOU IN?

Have you ever did something crazy and you thought you had learned that very same lesson numerous of times before? Your guard was up and you were now more focused on yourself instead of others. You have fast and prayed and there is no way the devil will get you with the same tricks that he has succeeded with in the past. Now you find you have uninvited guest and you're wondering to yourself **"WHO LET YOU IN"**?

As a child growing up in the south, we were accustom to leaving our front doors open and not worry about being robbed or being taking advantage of. Everyone in the neighborhood knew each other and everyone was pretty comfortable with each other.

However, as the sun began to go down and darkness approached, we were instructed to come inside of the house, close the doors, and lock them. If guest came to our home, they would knock on the door or ring the doorbell. Our response would be "who is it? The guest on the opposite side of the door would then identify themselves and our parents granted permission to open the door and welcome the guest into our home.

Well there was a knock at the door and you opened it without asking, "who is it"? We sometimes loose ourselves by focusing on the right things that we are doing and we forget the fact that our weaknesses sometimes speak much louder than our strengths.
The weak areas of our lives can be identified in many different ways. Our demeanor, our conversation, our guards being up to high, or sometimes just being a needy personality.

The enemy has now disguised itself as something you would enjoy or something that appeals to a weakness that you may have. You are not conscious that the enemy is using your weakness to destroy you. Yes your weakness is destroying you while you are enjoying yourself and indulging in a temporary gratification.

So remember whenever you hear someone knocking to gain access into your spiritual house. Make sure our "Father" has given you HIS permission for entrance. Make sure that all access into your spirit is protected. The enemy is seeking to devour us with the things we think we have conquered, but unconsciously we are vulnerable to it. By doing this, you will always know **"WHO LET YOU IN"?**

2 Corinthians 12:9 And he said unto me, My grace is sufficient for thee: for my strength is made perfect in weakness.

I Corinthians 10:13

2 Peter 2:9

YOUR PAIN HAS PURPOSE

Are you wondering how much more pain are you going to have to endure? What have you done to have caused such hurt to bombard your life? Is it necessary for one to continuously hurt with no relief? Be encouraged. The pain is only temporary. It has an assignment in your life. Yes **Your Pain Has Purpose.**

When we think of pain, we often think about it in a negative way. The reason for those thoughts is because of the discomfort or hurt that's associated with it. But, if we viewed our situation from a different perspective and see our pain as an opportunity for God to manifest his power through us, we may handle it differently.

Yes it is during our most painful moments in life that God uses as an opportunity to draw us closer to Him. We somehow have to find a way to reach out to Him and trust Him as we deal with the circumstances that we are presently facing.

In the book of Genesis, Who would have ever thought Joseph's pain would be instrumental in landing him in the palace? His pain had a purpose. It prepared him for what was ahead of him. Although going through the painful moments were difficult, he did not give up. He went through his process and received a promotion .

We to have to go through this moment in time fully assured that the Lord will see us through. We cannot allow the symptoms of an illness or the circumstances of our present situation dominate the fulfillment of what God has already spoken to be so. Just know this too shall pass because **Your Pain Has Purpose.**

Jeremiah 29:11 For I know the thoughts that I think towards you saith the Lord; thoughts of peace and not evil to give you an expected end.

Jeremiah 30:3

Isaiah 55:8

Romans 8:28

TURN TO THE WALL

Did you get up today ready to tackle the world and everything that could go wrong has hit you? Is it hard to find a hiding place and just cry within yourself? Do you find that so many have put demands on you, until you can't find you? The family, the job, the bills, the broken refrigerator, the broken plumbing, and your emotions are all screaming your name at the same time. Drop everything and **"TURN TO THE WALL"**.

Each day that God allow us to be introduced to is a blessing. Often times, difficult dilemmas can cloud over precious possibilities of embracing a wonderful day. It is easy for us to sit back and glide through life wishing for a stress free journey. The important thing that we must remember our day is designed by our very own way of thinking. As we speak positive things into our minds and our hearts, positive results will be the outcome.

The stresses and pressures of life can bombard us physically, mentally, emotionally, and spiritually. As you try to conquer all of these areas alone, it can become a very desolate place. It is very easy to find friends or loved ones to go out to dinner, but is very difficult to find someone to go to the valley with you.

Valleys are designed to perfect and prepare you for what is to come. But stay alert. The enemy will attack you with multiple attacks to break you down. Yes he has discussed your destiny and he wants to destroy you. He is after you with everything he has all at one time.

Yes God still has HIS hand upon you. Yes the eyes of the Lord are yet upon you. God designed you with purpose. Your members, HE fashioned and HE knows just how much you can handle. This valley time is a good time for you to get in position to be blessed for your labor and your faithfulness towards the Lord. This pain that you are facing is an instrument to lead you to a greater place in your life.

Pain has a way of leaving a memory that will ache every now and again as you excel in life. The ache is instrumental in helping you to remain humble and to keep the Lord as the center of your joy. It is never God's desire to bless you with greatness or trust you to carry His glory and it pulls your heart away from HIM into another direction. So this valley of sorrow is really a blessing for your tomorrow.

Rejoice in the valley alone. Encourage yourself. Utilize the wall. It is a place of refuge. It is a secret place for you to worship. So drop it all and **"TURN TO THE WALL"**.

2 King 20:1,2 set thine house in order for thou shalt die, and not live. V2 then he turned his face to the wall, and prayed unto the Lord…..

Psalms 46:1

Psalms 16:11

Psalms 42:1

THE WEALTH OF A REAL WOMAN

Have you ever felt devalued or miss-prized? Now that you have finally made up your mind to let go of that useless relationship, your ex tries to make you feel beneath him. I know sometimes we dive into relationships with our nose wide open and forget to keep one eye open. Such is life. Pick your head up and shake the dust off your feet. He was unable to recognize **THE WEALTH OF A REAL WOMAN.**

The time or era in which we live, materialistic things seems to supersede the qualities that are locked inside. We have a tendency to focus more on what a person can do for us monetarily and totally neglect what they can do for us within.

We have to make sure as real women, we do not allow our merchandise to be devalued. We have to know that our merchandise is good and it is under lock and key until God reveals the one in whom HE has entrusted to guard your wealth.

Please be assured that your wealth is not your bank statement. Your wealth is not the Gucci bag or St John suit in your closet. Your wealth is the treasures on the inside of you. The treasure on the inside of you is the substance that makes you virtuous and valuable. Your value is far above rubies because you possess qualities and substances on the inside that cannot be purchased.

It is very important as we journey through life that we do not mislabel our wealth. Society now has a anything goes mentality, but as woman of virtue we cannot allow our treasures to become contaminated. In our quest to be selected or fulfilled, we can sometimes lower our standards and settle for the wrong mate.

Stand your ground from this point on. The substance on the inside of you is valuable. You must guard your wealth with everything you have. The inner qualities carry way more weight than the outer. The outer is just a bunch of stuff. It is emptiness, null and void. It will eventually fade away, but your inner man will live with you forever. Hold on to your character, your morals, and your ethics for these things are priceless.

Celebrate the departure of that last relationship. Don't lose any more sleep and please enjoy eating a full course meal because he was not worthy of THE prize you are. He was unable to recognize **THE WEALTH OF A REAL WOMAN.**

Proverbs 31:10 Who can find a virtuous woman? For her price is far above rubies.

Proverbs 12:4

Proverbs 31: 25

Proverbs 4: 7

TIRED OF BEING COMFORTABLE

Do you get irritated and angry with yourself because you're not where you desire to be in life? Do you flare up inside as you watch others around you excel and you know you have the potential to do the same thing? Know that all is well. You are **"Tired Of Being Comfortable"**.

As you travel this journey of life in search of your destiny, do not submit to the negative seed called average living. Average living allows you the comfort of thinking you have accomplished a certain plateau in life beyond where you used to be and now you can sit back and relax because life is a little bit better than before.

In one's pursuit to reach certain goals in life, it is easy to lose sight on the bigger plan that God has in store for you. Instead of pressing and pursing the greatness that is inside of you, you allow yourself to be pacified with the ordinary when actually extraordinary has been destined for your life.

So as you focus on you, do not become irritated and angry because others around you are steadily moving forward. Turn those negative seeds into positive tools and allow this energy to work on your behalf. You are in control of you.

Yes the pacifier that is conveniently placed around your neck can no longer comfort the yearning that your soul is crying out for. Average living can no longer sustain the burning desire of excelling in life that is in side of you. Being comfortable is a good place to be, but it was not designed for your destiny. Pack your bags. It is time to move on because you are **"Tired of Being Comfortable"**.

Luke 5:4 Launch out into the deep, and let down your net for a draught.

John 14:12

Matthew 21:21

PERSONAL NOTES

Provoking Your Faith

THE END

Romona K. Stromas

www.ingramcontent.com/pod-product-compliance
Lightning Source LLC
LaVergne TN
LVHW051508070426
835507LV00022B/2985